A Mob of

Meerkats

Heinemann Library
Chicago, Illinois

Heidi Moore

© 2004 Reed Educational & Professional Publishing
Published by Heinemann Library,
a division of Reed Elsevier, Inc.,
Chicago, Illinois

Customer Service 888-454-2279

Visit our website at www.heinemannlibrary.com

Designed by Heinemann Library
Photo research by Bill Broyles
Originated at Dot Gradations, UK
Printed and bound in Hong Kong, China by Wing King Tong

08 07 06 05 04
10 9 8 7 6 5 4 3 2 1

Library of Congress Cataloging-in-Publication Data
Moore, Heidi, 1976-
  A mob of meerkats / Heidi Moore.
      p. cm. -- (Animal groups)
Summary: Describes the physical characteristics, behavior, habitat, and group life of meerkats.
Includes bibliographical references (p.   ).
  ISBN 1-4034-4694-6 (HC : lib. bdg.) 1-4034-5418-3 (PB)
  1. Meerkat--Juvenile literature. [1. Meerkat.] I. Title. II. Series.
  QL737.C235M66 2004
  599.74'2--dc21
                              2003010349

Acknowledgments
The author and publishers are grateful to the following for permission to reproduce copyright material:
title page, icons, p. 31 Corbis; pp. 4, 6, 25 Nigel J. Dennis/Gallo Images/Corbis; p. 5 Martin Harvey/Gallo Images/Corbis; p. 7 Marguerite Smits Van Oyen/Naturepl.com; p. 8 Peter Chadwick/Gallo Images/Corbis; p. 9 M. Harvey/DRK Photo; pp. 10, 20 Nigel J. Dennis/NHPA; pp. 11, 28 Tim Jackson/Oxford Scientific Films; p. 12 Peter Johnson/Corbis; pp. 13, 14, 15, 16, 17, 21, 23 David Macdonald/Oxford Scientific Films; p. 18 Clem Haagner/Photo Researchers, Inc.; p. 19 Nigel J. Dennis/Photo Researchers, Inc.; pp. 22, 27 Roberta Stacy; p. 24 Mark Bowler/NHPA; p. 26 Paul A. Souders/Corbis

Cover photograph by Marguerite Smits Van Oyen/Naturepl.com

The author would like to thank her husband, James, and her editor, Angela McHaney Brown.

The publisher would like to thank Dr. Steven W. Buskirk of the Department of Zoology and Physiology at the University of Wyoming for his comments in the preparation of this book.

Some words are shown in bold, **like this.** You can find out what they mean by looking in the glossary.

Contents

What Are Meerkats?

Meerkats are small, furry **mammals.** They live in a hot, dry area of southern Africa called the **savanna.** Meerkats are about 1 foot (30 centimeters) long, not including the tail. They weigh less than 2 pounds (900 grams). They have long, thin tails that are almost as long as their bodies. Male and female meerkats look basically the same, but the females are larger. Meerkats can stand on all four feet or on just their hind legs.

Meerkats have shaggy, reddish-brown or tan fur with dark brown bands along their backs. Their ears and tails have black tips. They have narrow, pointed **snouts** and a very good sense of smell. Meerkats, which are also known as suricates, live up to twelve years in the wild.

Meerkats' tails help them balance on their long hind legs.

4

In the family

Meerkats are in the mongoose family. Mongooses live in underground homes called burrows or in other sheltered places. Mongooses are very fierce hunters.

Groups of meerkats

Meerkats are **social** animals. Although each meerkat does some things alone, it spends most of its time in a group with other meerkats. A group of meerkats is called a mob. In this book we will look at how mobs of meerkats live together in the wild.

Meerkats have brown or tan fur, dark bands on their backs, and light-colored fur on their bellies.

Where Do Meerkats Live?

Meerkats live in the dry **savannas** and deserts of South Africa, Botswana, Namibia, and Angola. Much of this area is covered with **scrub,** or grasses and short bushes. The soil is rocky or sandy. Temperatures there can be very hot during the summer—as high as 122 ˚F (50 ˚C). But during the winter, nighttime temperatures can drop to freezing.

Like the other plants and animals of the savanna, meerkats have **adapted** to the **habitat** in which they live. Meerkats find food, shelter, and everything they need to survive there. They have dark rings beneath their eyes that act as sunglasses to help them see in the bright sunlight of the savanna.

Each meerkat mob lives within a home **range.** Most ranges are 2 to 6 square miles (5 to 16 square kilometers). Meerkats move around within this range to find food.

Meerkats live in hot, dry places such as the Kalahari Desert.

The savanna is often hot, but it can get cold at night. Meerkats warm up by stretching out in the morning sun.

Where Do Meerkats Sleep?

Meerkats are **diurnal**, which means they are active during the day. When it is time to sleep, they find shelter in an underground **burrow**, in a log, or in spaces between rocks. Most of the time meerkats use their long, sharp claws to dig their own burrows. When they dig, they close their ears so dirt and sand cannot get in. Burrows are usually lined with grass and can be up to 10 feet (3 meters) deep.

Meerkats have four sharp claws on each of their feet. They can dig their entire body weight in sand in just minutes!

Meerkats sleep in a furry pile in the burrow to stay warm at night when temperatures drop.

A mob has several burrows within its home **range** so all of its members can duck underground quickly when there is danger. Sometimes meerkats share these burrows with other animals that live in the **savanna**, such as ground squirrels or yellow mongooses. Sometimes meerkats sleep in burrows dug by other animals.

What Happens in a Mob?

Meerkats are **social** animals. They work together, play together, and sleep together. Sometimes they even fight **predators** together. Working together helps them find enough food and stay safe. Each member of the mob has a different job to do, just as humans do. Sometimes meerkats have more than one job.

Members of a meerkat mob take time out to play.

Members of the mob

A meerkat mob has as few as three and as many as thirty members. Most mobs have ten to fifteen meerkats. Each mob is led by a **dominant** pair of male and female meerkats. They are usually bigger than the other members of the mob.

Meerkats are very friendly with members of their own mob, but they are hostile toward other mobs. Because meerkats look so similar, it is often difficult to tell one from another. So a meerkat must rely on **scent markings** to recognize a member of its mob. Meerkats have scent glands near their hind ends, which they use to mark one another as well as their **territory.** If one meerkat does not recognize another meerkat's scent, it knows the other meerkat is not a member of the same mob. Then it may attack.

Meerkats also use scent marking as a form of bonding, or being social.

11

Do meerkats talk to each other?

Meerkats in a mob need to **communicate** with each other. They use different sounds to get across different messages. When they are cuddling close, as a mother and a baby do, they make a purring noise. They also stay in close contact when they hunt, using a kind of chattering call.

Members of a mob also make sounds when they are scared or angry. When a meerkat senses danger, it makes a loud cry or bark to warn the others. When facing **predators**, meerkats hiss and growl. In all, meerkats make more than ten different sounds.

Meerkats communicate with one another while they are searching for food.

Another way meerkats communicate is through touch. Meerkats are very affectionate. Young and old meerkats alike spend time **grooming** each other. In the morning, meerkats groom each other while they warm up in the sun. They especially like grooming at the base of the tail.

These meerkats are taking a break from a busy day to groom. Sometimes a meerkat will eat the tick or flea it finds in another's fur. Other **mammals**, such as gorillas and chimps, do the same.

What Jobs Do Meerkats Have?

Staying alive is a difficult task in the **savanna.** Meerkats have a lot to do, from finding food to raising **pups.** There are many jobs for members of a meerkat mob.

Sentry

Some meerkats serve as **sentries,** or lookouts, watching for danger. They keep watch on a high rock or in the branches of a tree. If they see a **predator,** they make a sound to warn the others. Meerkats' good eyesight helps them watch for predators. They can see an eagle up to about 1,000 feet (300 meters) away.

A meerkat mob relies on sentries like this one to watch for predators while the others look for food.

Babysitter

Some of the most important members of a mob are the babysitters. A new mother has to find food, or she will starve. While she is hunting, she leaves her pups with another adult female. Meerkat babysitters feed the pups and protect them from harm, just as human babysitters do. Babysitters snuggle close to the pups to keep them warm. With the extra body heat, young meerkats can focus on doing what they do best—growing.

Risking their lives

Babysitters can lose up to two percent of their body weight in one day of not eating! But they still do their part to help the pups grow strong and healthy while the other members of the mob hunt.

Meerkats go to a lot of trouble to take care of each other. While a meerkat is babysitting, it cannot **mate**. It also cannot find food of its own. But taking care of the **pups** helps out the whole group. In this way, meerkats seem to care more about the good of the mob than any single animal.

A babysitter snuggles close to a group of pups to keep them warm.

Why Do Meerkats Work Together?

All members of a mob must **cooperate** in order to survive. Mobs with fewer than five members have a more difficult time surviving. With only a few members, there are not enough meerkats to do all the jobs. The meerkats in small groups are too busy finding food to do **sentry** duty. If any one meerkat were to spend too much time on guard duty instead of hunting, it would starve. So small groups live without sentries. Without a guard always looking out for **predators**, it is more likely that meerkats in these smaller groups will be killed.

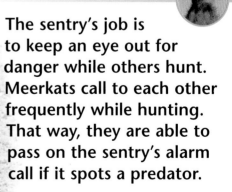

The sentry's job is to keep an eye out for danger while others hunt. Meerkats call to each other frequently while hunting. That way, they are able to pass on the sentry's alarm call if it spots a predator.

17

Together is better

Larger groups survive better because there are more meerkats to share the work. Groups with fifteen to thirty meerkats survive best. The larger the group, the more meerkats there are to keep watch and to guard the **pups.** Big groups also are better at keeping other mobs out of their **range.** It is important for one mob to keep other mobs away so they do not have to share the same food supply.

A meerkat mob will fight other mobs to **defend** its home range.

The size of a meerkat mob changes over time. When some members leave in order to find their own **mates** or start their own mob, the group gets smaller. The mob also gets smaller when members die. But when pups are born, or when meerkats from another mob join them, the mob gets bigger.

A mob of meerkats may change over time, but its members are very loyal to one another.

19

What Do Meerkats Eat?

Meerkats spend five to eight hours every day hunting. They **forage** for food, pressing their noses close to the ground and rooting through the soil. Their good sense of smell comes in handy for sniffing out insects or rodents in the dirt. Then they use their claws to dig in the sand to capture the **prey**. Meerkats are **carnivores**, which means they eat mostly animals. They eat spiders, snails, insects, and **larvae**. The also eat lizards, rodents, and birds that nest on the ground.

A keen sense of smell and sharp claws are the only tools a meerkat needs to find a meal.

Meerkats must spend most of each day foraging for food or they will starve. If they do not find enough food in one area, they will move on to another place.

It is often dry in the **savanna**, so sources of water like rivers and lakes are hard to find. Meerkats usually get all the water they need by eating such plant parts as roots and bulbs. Plants are a good source of water.

This meerkat just captured a tasty scorpion. Scorpion poison does not seem to affect meerkats. With their sharp teeth, meerkats can gobble up scorpions and other stinging insects quickly, before getting stung.

21

Meerkats **mate** about once a year. Usually the **dominant** male and female are the ones that mate. Most of the **pups** born in each mob—about eight out of ten—are from the dominant pair. In the wild, meerkats mate during the wet season. There can be two to five pups in a **litter,** but there are usually four. Meerkats give birth in the **burrow.**

Pups are born hairless and blind, so their mothers must stay close to protect and feed them. After their eyes open, they can come out of the burrow.

22

Growing up

After about three weeks, pups have grown enough to leave the burrow, but they are still too young to stray very far. Pups are curious and require a lot of attention.

Meerkats are **mammals**, so they **suckle** milk from their mother. Meerkat mothers need to **forage** constantly to keep up their milk supply. They suckle their young for six to nine weeks.

A meerkat stands on her hind legs to suckle her two pups.

23

Who cares for the pups?

Every member of the mob helps out with the **pups.** A mother teaches her pups to hunt. She runs around with food in her mouth and waits for the pups to snatch it from her. When a meerkat mother leaves the **burrow** to **forage**, she leaves her pups with a babysitter. While she is away, the pups are active. They play, fight, and compete for the babysitter's attention. Older brothers and sisters help out by **grooming**, guarding, and playing with the pups.

Playing helps young meerkats learn the skills they will need when they are older, such as foraging, fighting, and self-defense. After eighteen months, meerkats are completely grown. They are now old enough to take on new roles in the mob.

A young meerkat has much to learn in order to survive.

Do Meerkats Fight?

Meerkats fight for many reasons. Pups in the same mob play-fight, or pretend to fight each other, to learn important self-defense skills. Sometimes meerkats fight to prove their strength. Larger, more aggressive meerkats become leaders of the mob, and weaker meerkats become less **dominant.**

Teeth bared and tails up, meerkat pups fight to win dominance in the mob.

Sometimes meerkats fight other mobs over their land, or **territory.** Food is hard to find, especially when there is little rain. So meerkats sometimes try to take over each other's **ranges** to increase their food supply. Then the mobs will face off and try to drive each other away from the range. Eventually one mob will be forced to leave, and the other will take over the territory.

Meerkats are small animals, so they have many **predators** in the **savanna**. These predators include eagles, vultures, and jackals. Cobras and other snakes try to eat meerkat **pups**.

Meerkats would rather run away than face danger. When a predator such as an eagle or a jackal approaches, meerkats run away quickly with their tails up. But if they cannot run away, meerkats may make a **mock**, or pretend, attack.

Sentries look far into the distance to watch for predators such as this black-backed jackal.

What happens in a mock attack?

In a mock attack, meerkats make themselves look more fierce. First they dig up the ground to make clouds of dust. This makes it hard for the predator to see. Then the meerkats move forward in a group to try to scare away the predator. Some of them jump in the air and growl fiercely. Some of the stronger meerkats may bite the predator until it goes away.

It is best for groups of meerkats to stick together when danger is near.

Staying alive

If a predator does not go away, a meerkat has to defend itself. It crouches on the ground on its back with its teeth bared and claws out.

A rough life

Only one in four meerkats makes it to adulthood. Some are killed by **predators**. Others die from starvation. When the **savanna** becomes too dry to support the animals that meerkats eat, the mob is forced to find a new **range**. To find food, they often have to travel far from home, where the danger of predators is greater.

Meerkats and humans

When humans move into land where meerkats live, they threaten the meerkats' **habitat**. As some of the most **social mammals**, meerkats are very good at working together. By studying them, people can learn more about **cooperation**. But we can learn from them only if we protect their habitat.

 As people continue to harm the environment, it becomes difficult for animals such as meerkats to survive in the wild.

Meerkat Facts

Where do meerkats live?

Meerkats live in southern Africa in the area shown on the map.

Key
☐ Meerkats

AFRICA

equator

Atlantic Ocean

Indian Ocean

What other animals live in the savanna?

The African savanna is home to a lot of animals. Lions, giraffes, zebras, gerbils, aardvarks, and bat-eared foxes are some of the animals that share the dry savanna with meerkats.

How do meerkats keep cool?

Even though meerkats live in mostly dry areas, they love bathing when water is available. It helps them cool off. During the hottest part of the day, meerkats try to stay out of the sun. They rest in the shade, play, or **groom** each other. Also, meerkats' small size helps them stay cool. Smaller animals lose heat faster than large ones, so meerkats are not likely to overheat in the hot desert. But that also means meerkats have to snuggle close in the **burrow** to stay warm when desert temperatures drop at night.

How well do meerkats see?

Meerkats have very good eyesight, which helps **sentries** spot a predator such as a martial eagle in the distance. But their close-up vision is not as good. Sometimes they cannot see food directly in front of them. Meerkats rely on their keen sense of smell.

Glossary

adapt change over time to fit in with the environment

burrow hole or tunnel dug by an animal for shelter

carnivore animal that mostly eats other animals

communicate pass on information to another

cooperate work together

defend protect from danger or attack

diurnal active during the day

dominant refers to the leader or most important member of a group

forage search for food

groom when one animal cleans bits of dirt, dead skin, or insects from the hair of another animal

habitat place where an animal or plant lives

larva (more than one are called larvae) early form of an insect

litter young animals produced by an animal at one time

mammal hairy, warm-blooded animal that feeds its young with milk from the mother's body

mate joining of a male and female of the same species to create young; or, partner for creating young

mock not real

predator animal that hunts other animals for food

prey animal that is hunted and eaten by another animal

pup newborn or young meerkat

range area of land in which a group of animals lives and hunts

savanna area of flat grassland with few trees

scent marking smell that identifies members of a group

scrub short trees or bushes

sentry one who serves as a lookout

snout long nose that sticks out from the rest of the face

social living in a group

suckle drink milk from a mother's body

territory particular area of land that a group of animals claims as its own

Longman, Christina. *African Grasslands*. Columbus, Ohio: McGraw-Hill, 2001.

Peterson, David. *Africa*. Danbury, Conn.: Children's Press, 1998.

Robinson, W. Wright. *How Mammals Build Their Amazing Homes*. Farmington, Hills, Mich.: Gale Group, 1999.

Unwin, Mike. *The Life Cycle of Mammals*. Chicago: Heinemann, 2003.

Weaver, Robyn. *Meerkats*. Mankato, Minn.: Capstone, 1998.

Index